ASTROLOGY

AQUARIUS

BY ABBY DOTY

Apex is distributed by North Star Editions:
sales@northstareditions.com | 888-417-0195

Produced for Apex by Red Line Editorial.

Photographs ©: Shutterstock Images, cover (illustration, constellation), cover (background), 1, 4–5, 6, 7 (background), 8–9, 10–11, 12–13, 14, 16–17, 18–19, 20, 21, 22–23, 25, 26–27, 29; iStockphoto, 7 (constellation)

Library of Congress Control Number: 2025939146

ISBN
979-8-89250-780-6 (hardcover)
979-8-89250-809-4 (paperback)
979-8-89250-866-7 (ebook pdf)
979-8-89250-838-4 (hosted ebook)

Printed in the United States of America
Mankato, MN
012026

NOTE TO PARENTS AND EDUCATORS

Apex books are designed to build literacy skills in striving readers. Exciting, high-interest content attracts and holds readers' attention. The text is carefully leveled to allow students to achieve success quickly. Additional features, such as bolded glossary words for difficult terms, help build comprehension.

TABLE OF CONTENTS

CHAPTER 1

WATER BEARER

Aquarius is a large **constellation**. It is made up of many stars. People say the stars show a man. He is pouring water from a jug. In Latin, Aquarius means "water bearer."

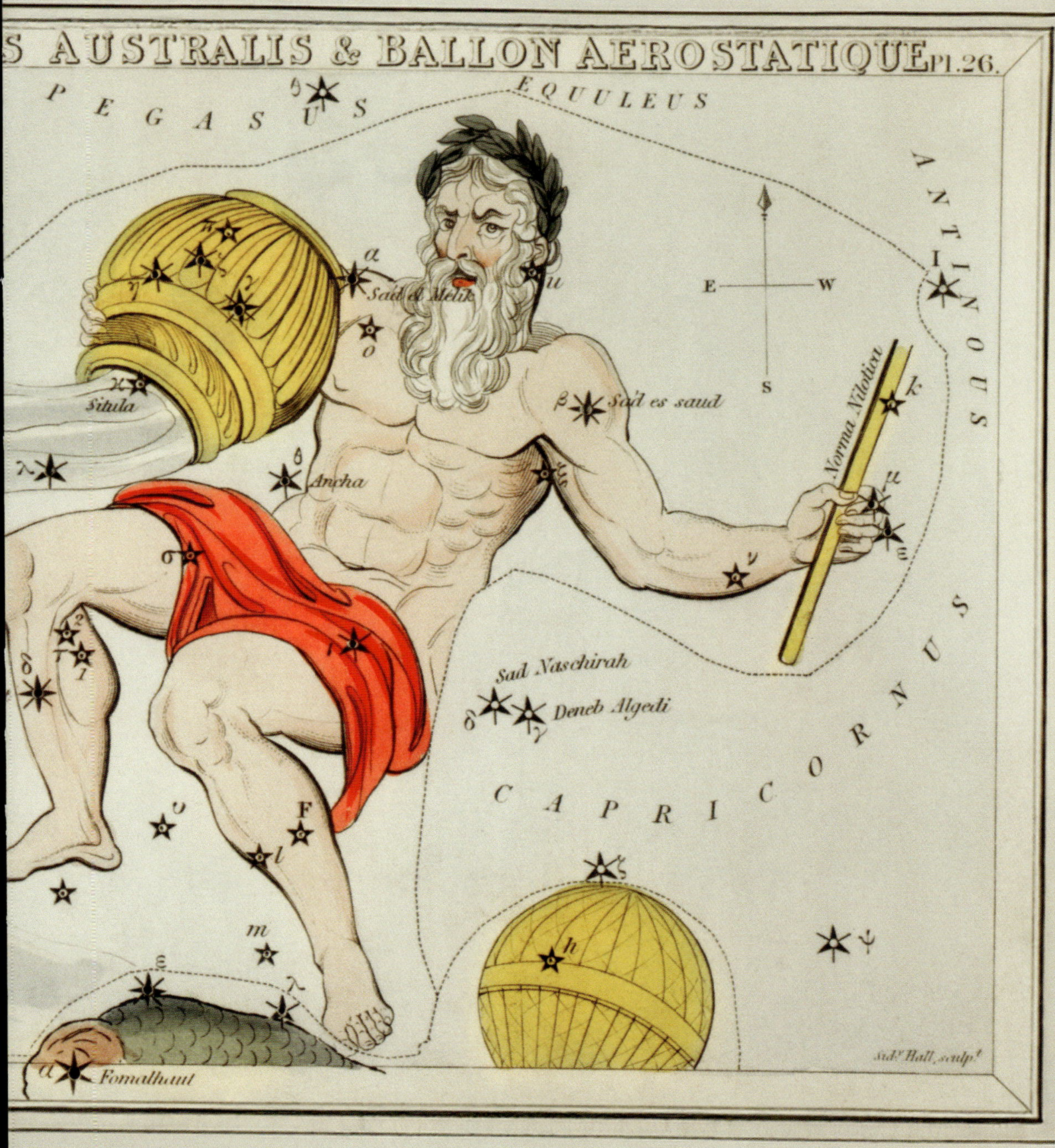

Aquarius includes hundreds of stars. But only a few of them are bright.

Ptolemy spent years studying planets and stars. He made a list of 48 constellations.

A Greek **astronomer** studied the constellation. His name was Ptolemy. He wrote about it in the 100s CE.

FAST FACT

People in Babylon had a constellation similar to Aquarius. They said it showed their water god, Ea.

People connect the stars in Aquarius to make several bent lines.

People told **myths** about Aquarius. Some said the jug of water created large floods. Others linked the water with life and healing.

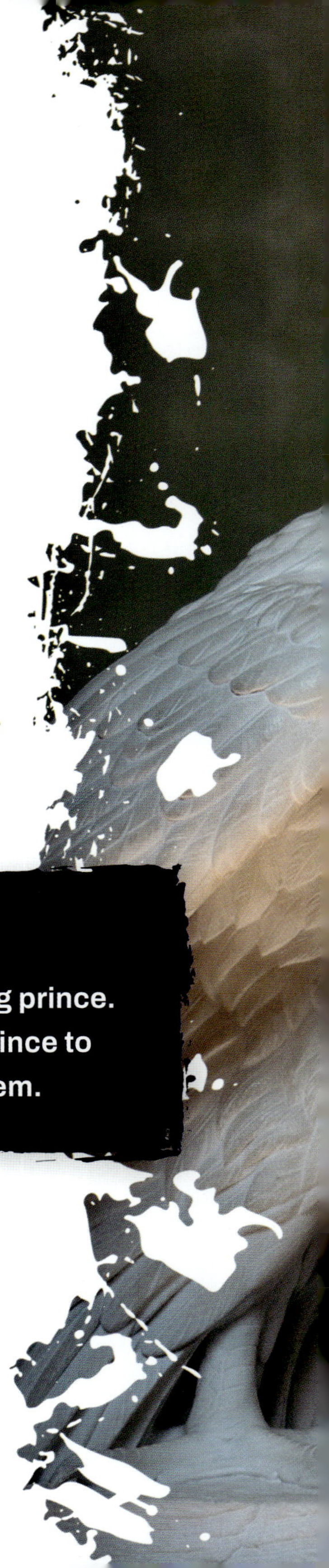

GREEK MYTH

One Greek myth said the water bearer was a young prince. The god Zeus took the prince. Zeus brought the prince to live with the gods. The prince poured drinks for them.

A Greek myth says Zeus turned into an eagle to capture a young prince named Ganymede.

CHAPTER 2

A STARRY CYCLE

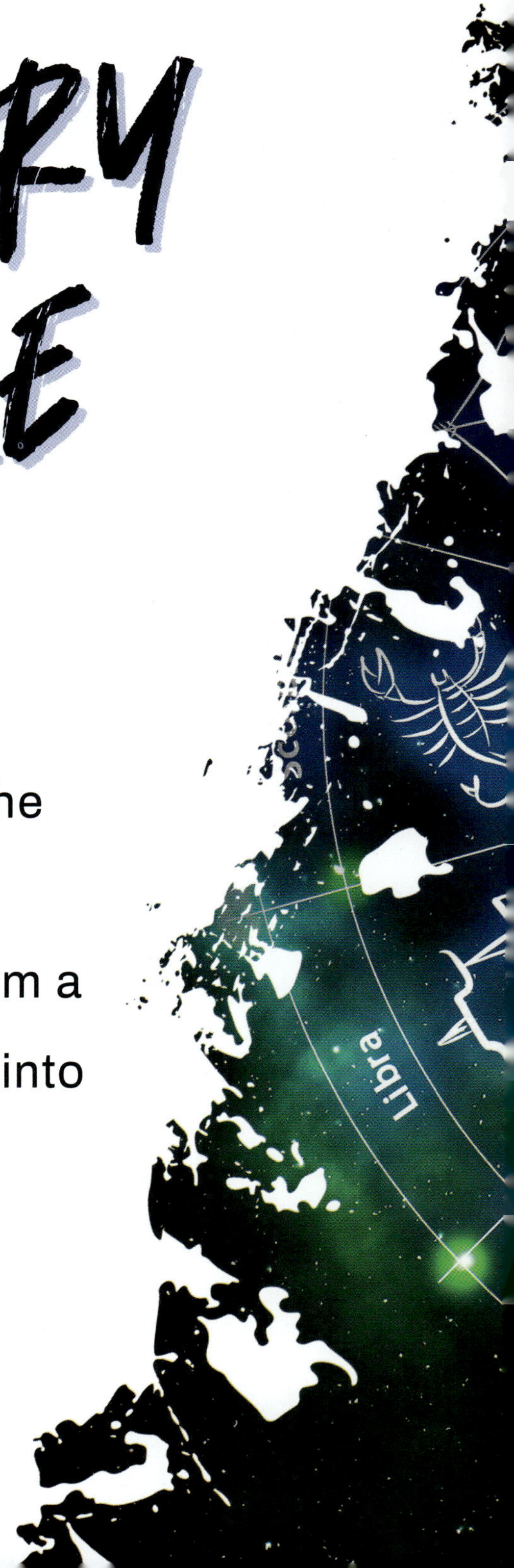

Aquarius is one of the 12 **zodiac** signs. Together, these signs form a cycle. It divides the year into 12 parts.

Each zodiac sign is based on a different constellation.

Aquarius's time is matched with winter. This season can be a time to think or dream.

Aquarius is the 11th sign in the cycle. Its time starts around January 20. It ends around February 18. People born during this time are called Aquarians.

FAST FACT

The zodiac cycle begins in March. Aries is the first sign.

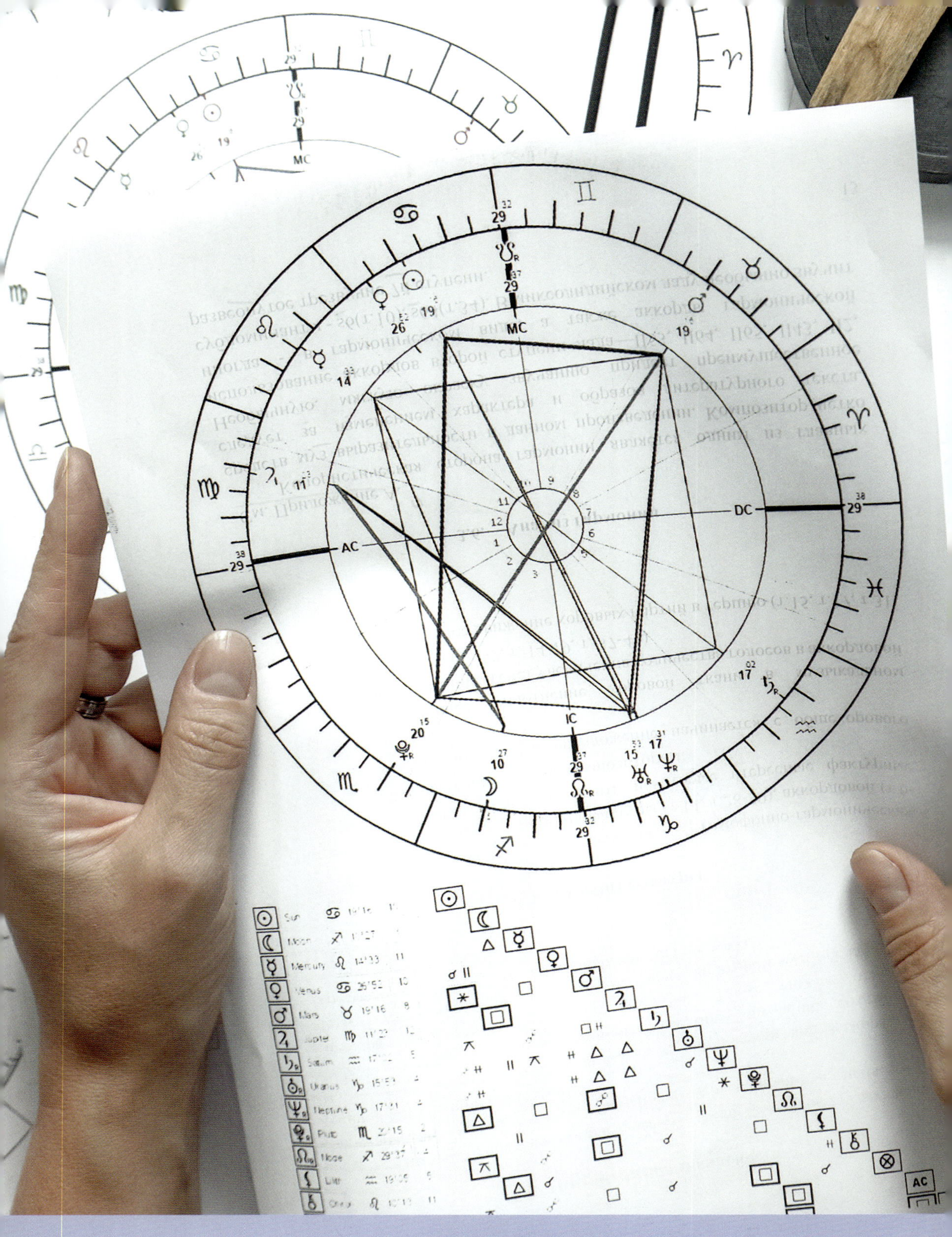

In astrology, zodiac signs are said to shape people's lives. So is the **element** that each sign gets matched with. Aquarius's element is air.

HOROSCOPES

Some people read horoscopes. Horoscope writers look at the movement of the moon and planets. They suggest what people might do or feel as a result. They often give different tips based on people's **sun signs**.

People can use charts to find their signs, which are based on when they were born.

CHAPTER 3

ABOUT AQUARIUS

In astrology, people often use two squiggly lines to represent Aquarius. This **glyph** looks like waves of water.

Some people say the lines in Aquarius's glyph represent the flow of ideas and energy.

However, Aquarius is one of the three air signs. People with air signs are said to be smart and social. They may also be leaders or deep thinkers.

FAST FACT

Gemini and Libra are the other air signs.

In astrology, each element is paired with three zodiac signs.

The planet Uranus is tilted on its side. In astrology, it stands for being unique.

Uranus is the ruling planet for Aquarius. This planet is said to shape how Aquarians act. It is linked to change and new ideas.

NEW RULER

Long ago, Aquarius's ruling planet was Saturn. That planet represents order. But people discovered Uranus in 1781. It became Aquarius's modern ruler.

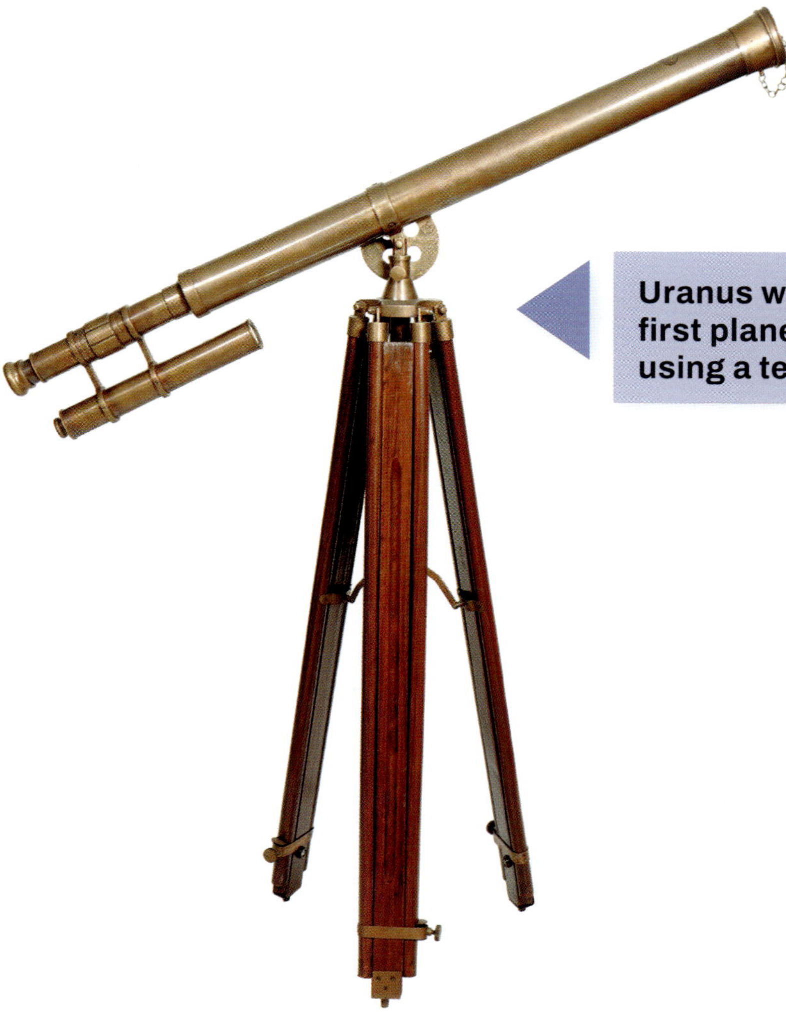

Uranus was the first planet found using a telescope.

CHAPTER 4

COMMON TRAITS

In astrology, Aquarians are said to have several **traits**. One is being creative. They may like making art or inventing things.

Aquarians are known for expressing their thoughts and feelings in art.

Another trait is being independent. That can mean thinking for themselves rather than following others. Or it can mean having just a small group of friends.

FAST FACT

Famous Aquarians include Harry Styles, Cristiano Ronaldo, and Michael B. Jordan.

Aquarians may dress or act in ways that make them stand out. ▶

Aquarians may be drawn to jobs that involve helping others, such as being doctors.

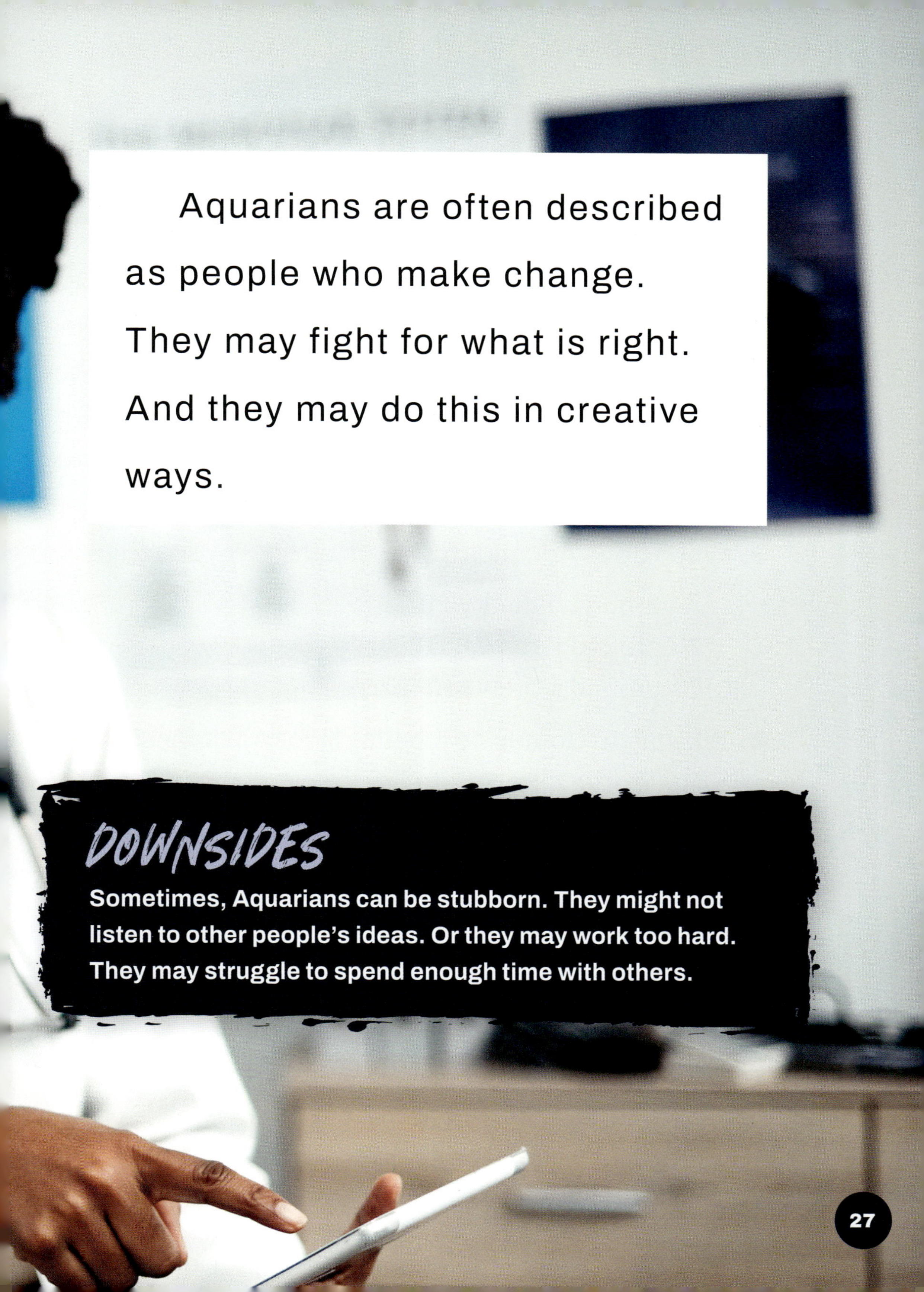

Aquarians are often described as people who make change. They may fight for what is right. And they may do this in creative ways.

DOWNSIDES

Sometimes, Aquarians can be stubborn. They might not listen to other people's ideas. Or they may work too hard. They may struggle to spend enough time with others.

COMPREHENSION QUESTIONS

Write your answers on a separate piece of paper.

1. Write a few sentences explaining the main ideas of Chapter 4.

2. Do you ever read horoscopes? Why or why not?

3. When does Aquarius's season start?

- **A.** around January 20
- **B.** around February 18
- **C.** around March 11

4. Why might Uranus be a better fit for Aquarians' ruling planet than Saturn?

- **A.** because Saturn represents change, which Aquarians dislike
- **B.** because Uranus represents order, which Aquarians love
- **C.** because both Uranus and Aquarians have ties to change

5. What does **cycle** mean in this book?

Together, these signs form a ***cycle****. It divides the year into 12 parts.*

- **A.** a set of things that form a pattern
- **B.** a set of facts that no one knows
- **C.** a group of words in a sentence

6. What does **stubborn** mean in this book?

Sometimes, Aquarians can be ***stubborn****. They might not listen to other people's ideas.*

- **A.** willing to change how one thinks or acts
- **B.** not willing to change how one thinks or acts
- **C.** ready to listen to others

Answer key on page 32.

GLOSSARY

astronomer
A person who studies objects in space.

constellation
A group of stars that form a shape.

element
One of four forces (air, earth, fire, or water) that each zodiac sign is matched with and said to be shaped by.

glyph
A shape that stands for a word or idea.

myths
Well-known stories from the past that often include magic.

sun signs
People's main zodiac signs, which are decided by their birth dates.

traits
Ways that people look, think, or act.

zodiac
The set of 12 signs used in astrology, based on a part of the sky that the sun appears to move through each year.

TO LEARN MORE

BOOKS

Goldstein, Margaret J. *Mysteries of Stars*. Lerner Publications, 2021.

Loh-Hagan, Virginia. *Chinese Zodiac.* Cherry Lake Publishing, 2021.

Loh-Hagan, Virginia. *Star Signs*. Cherry Lake Publishing, 2021.

ONLINE RESOURCES

Visit **www.apexeditions.com** to find links and resources related to this title.

ABOUT THE AUTHOR

Abby Doty is a writer, editor, and booklover from Minnesota. Her sun sign is Aquarius.

INDEX

ANSWER KEY:
1. Answers will vary; 2. Answers will vary; 3. A; 4. C; 5. A; 6. B